The GROWN-UP'S GUIDE to CRAFTING WITH KIDS

20+ FUN AND EASY CRAFT PROJECTS TO INSPIRE YOU AND THE LITTLE ONES IN YOUR LIFE

Vicki Manning

Walter Foster

© 2020 Quarto Publishing Group USA Inc.
Artwork and text © 2020 Vicki Manning

First published in 2020 by Walter Foster Publishing, an imprint of The Quarto Group. 26391 Crown Valley Parkway, Suite 220, Mission Viejo, CA 92691, USA.
T (949) 380-7510 F (949) 380-7575 **www.QuartoKnows.com**

Walter Foster Publishing titles are also available at discount for retail, wholesale, promotional, and bulk purchase. For details, contact the Special Sales Manager by email at specialsales@quarto.com or by mail at The Quarto Group, Attn: Special Sales Manager, 100 Cummings Center, Suite 265D, Beverly, MA 01915, USA.

ISBN: 978-1-63322-860-3

Digital edition published in 2020
eISBN: 978-1-63322-861-0

In-House Editor: Annika Geiger

Printed in China
10 9 8 7 6 5 4 3 2 1

TABLE OF CONTENTS

INTRODUCTION

Crafting offers a wonderful way to get creative with children. But where to start? You may have seen about 101 different projects online and feel totally overwhelmed, causing you to wonder: Are they easy enough for my child to do? Will I need lots of expensive tools and materials? Do I need to be an expert in woodwork, sewing, pottery, or something else?

In this book, I will show you how—with the help of a basic toolkit, some key techniques, and step-by-step projects—you can get crafty with your children, without extra stress or expense. I've put together a handy guide to tools and materials, as well as more than 25 simple projects and creative prompts that were tested by my own children and are guaranteed to spark joy in your life as well! With this book, you and the kids you love can create lots of keepsakes to proudly display in your home or give as gifts to someone special. Even better, you'll also have the treasured memories of your creative time together. Come and join me on a crafting adventure!

WHY CRAFT?

BONDING Crafting offers a fantastic opportunity to spend dedicated and focused time with children. They will appreciate the one-on-one time and relish the opportunity to create something with you.

FINE-MOTOR SKILLS Crafting improves kids' dexterity because it requires them to use their fingers and hands. Drawing, cutting, gluing, threading—these are skills that help kids develop and improve their hand-eye coordination.

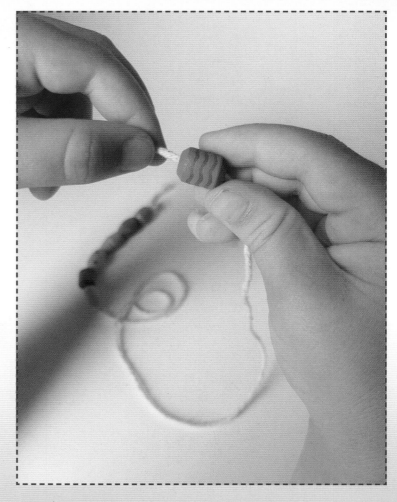

MINDFULNESS Creative activities are good for mental health. Sharing these activities with your child can be a very relaxing and rewarding experience for both of you.

SELF-EXPRESSION Giving options and choices when deciding what to craft together is a great way to help children express themselves. If the craft features embellishments, such as buttons and beads, I like to give my children a small selection so they can choose what to use. Consider offering color choices or prompting kids to think about which materials would be best for a certain activity.

CONFIDENCE Creating something gives kids a great sense of achievement and pride and demonstrates to them that they are capable of successfully following instructions. Whenever possible, try to encourage your child to take control during crafting sessions and avoid suggesting how to make changes to their creations.

GETTING STARTED

Make sure you have all of the necessary materials on hand before starting a craft. Read through the steps—and then read them again to make sure you haven't missed anything. It may sound obvious, but many times I've started a project and then had to stop to rummage for a material, and by the time I got back to my craft, my kids had lost interest and wandered off! In the step-by-step projects in this book, I provide lists and photos of what you will need before you get started so that you can avoid the same thing happening to you!

PROTECT YOUR CLOTHES & FURNITURE I recommend investing in an apron to wear over your clothes, or if you have old T-shirts lying around, those will work too. Save newspapers or magazines for covering work surfaces. If you use materials that may cause stains, such as permanent markers or colored tissue paper, I advise placing a cheap tray under your crafting project. It's an awful feeling to have created something beautiful with your child but ruined your new table in the process!

BE REALISTIC You may love the idea of a craft but have doubts as to whether your child has the skills to do it. Trust your instincts. If you think it might be difficult, it probably will be. You will most likely struggle to keep your child's attention, which will cause frustration in both of you. Crafting is meant to be enjoyable and rewarding! Giving kids something that's easier for them to do will free them up to express their creativity and help them gain confidence in their abilities.

TOOLS & MATERIALS

I consider the following items essential resources for crafting with children. You don't need to go out and buy everything at once, but if you have these items, you will be ready to make most of the crafts in this book—and you will be able to continue crafting together for years to come!

SCISSORS I use a larger pair for cardboard and paper and a smaller pair of craft scissors for cutting ribbon and fabric. When crafting with younger children, you might want to give them a pair of safety scissors and be selective about what you let them cut until their cutting skills are more developed.

GLUE & TAPE

- **PVA** Can be used with card stock, paper, fabric, and natural objects.

- **GLUE STICK** A medium-sized glue stick one is easy for your child to hold while also providing decent coverage, and it's useful for gluing paper and card stock together, as it dries quickly.

- **HOT-GLUE GUN** Kids should use this only under close supervision. I recommend selecting a smaller gun, as it generates less glue when you squeeze the trigger, making it much easier to control.

- **MASKING & WASHI TAPE** Both types work well for children to achieve good results quickly. I prefer masking and washi tape over clear tape because clear tape tears more easily, and masking and washi tape can be painted over.

PAPER I have a plastic tub dedicated to paper: gift wrap from birthday parties, interesting gift bags, magazine cutouts, and even wallpaper samples go in there! If you'd like to build up your own supply of paper resources, I recommend including tissue paper in a variety of colors (you can buy a mixed pack).

CARD STOCK It's helpful to have colorful card stock on hand, but cereal boxes also make an excellent source of cardboard and can be painted to suit your project. Other useful sources of card stock include paper-towel rolls, greeting cards, and boxes.

PAINT PENS Great for detailed work and extremely versatile, paint pens can be used on most surfaces, including wood, ceramic, and glass. Fine-tip markers make a good substitute. You can buy both in a multipack of mixed colors.

POM-POMS, PIPE CLEANERS, FEATHERS & GOOGLY EYES Useful for adding features to animals as well as for making bugs. A small bag of each is perfect. Try to get a multicolor pack so that it can be used for a variety of crafts; you can normally pick these up in craft stores and online.

CRAFT KNIFE Allow only older children to use this—with your supervision. A craft knife is very useful for detailed cutting as well as to cut out the center of an object. Place a cutting board underneath the item, and try to find one with a ruler to help guide you.

ADDITIONAL ITEMS You will also need paint, pencils, and felt-tip pens. A few of the projects in this book require more specific tools and materials, but these can usually be found online. I suggest alternatives whenever possible.

Something I find extremely useful for crafting is a good selection of everyday objects, natural items, and recycled materials that can be repurposed for crafting. You can get the whole family involved in building up a collection and have a lot of fun in the process!

NATURE

Whenever you and your kids go on a hike together, visit the beach, or even just play at the park, spend some time collecting natural objects. You can gradually build up a nice collection that will inspire your creative activities—and kids love bringing the outside indoors!

Choose a home for your natural treasures (my children use an old candy jar) and ensure that everything is clean, dry, and free of bugs before storing. The wonderful thing about sourcing materials from the outside is that your collection will constantly change depending on the time of year and your location. Plus, you and your kids will enjoy the many health benefits that come from spending time outdoors, including exercise and fresh air!

Examples: pine cones, feathers, shells, rocks, twigs, leaves, nuts, seeds, bark, and flowers

There's so much potential for spontaneous creativity: seeds for fairies' hats, pine-cone animals, acorn people, and much more. Ask your children for their ideas and let their imaginations run wild!

We made this little owl from felt and nature finds. His eyes are acorn shells, to which we added the pupils with marker. We attached the feathers, felt, and acorn caps with PVA glue.

Collecting nature finds is a great opportunity to build your child's vocabulary. Talk about the names of your finds and where they came from!

Next time you go on a walk together, pack strips of heavy paper or card stock, attach double-sided tape to the entire length of each strip, and have your child collect interesting-looking natural objects. I always encourage my children not to pick wildflowers and instead to collect "found" objects, such as fallen leaves and weeds with broken stems.

If the weather allows, take your crafting outside. It will make cleanup easier, and being surrounded by the great outdoors can help inspire your child's creativity!

Once you have finished collecting, peel back the tape and attach your finds. Leave each end of the tape free so that the card stock or paper can be placed around your child's head like a crown and the ends taped together.

Now your child will have a lovely nature crown to wear during your adventures together!

Sometimes all you need to transform your natural objects are paint and glue. My son wanted to paint some sycamore seeds and sticks, so we used them to create a dragonfly. Seeds and sticks work well for creating insect wings and bodies.

Sticks can be used to create a miniature loom. To make the frame, just wrap string in a figure eight at each corner of the frame; then secure each corner with a knot. Loop string around two of the sides to create the vertical threads. My kids and I enjoyed collecting flowers, grasses, and leaves to weave through our natural loom. There's no "right" way to do this, making it the perfect creative craft for children of all ages.

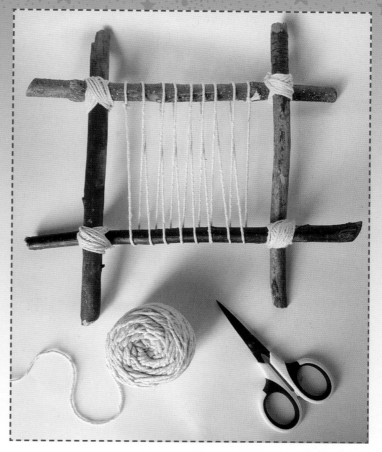

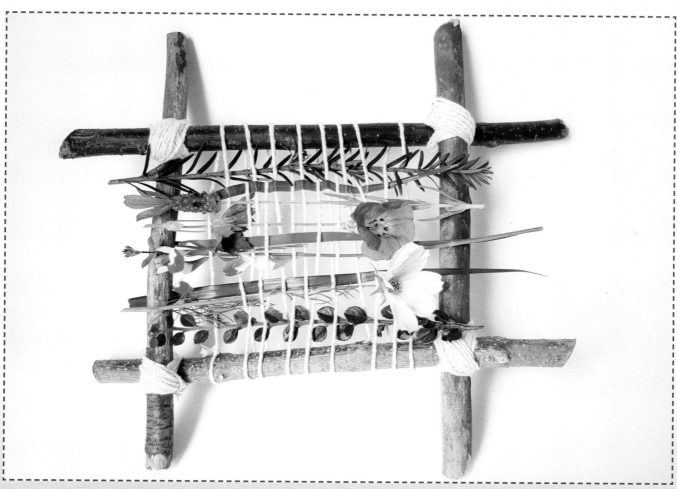

A visit to the beach can provide an abundance of resources! We had lots of fun finding these treasures and now have a ready source of free supplies for crafting. Make sure you give your beach finds a good wash and dry before storing.

Rocks make another great, readily available source of crafting inspiration. If you don't have access to mountains or the beach, visit your local gardening store. My kids and I use a combination of pebbles from the beach, stones from the gardening store, and glass pebbles purchased online.

We love to create story stones onto which we glue pictures from my kids' favorite books. Another option is to draw directly on the rocks using paint pens. We found these black rocks during our summer vacation, and they worked perfectly for a space theme!

How about getting together as a family and painting some pet rocks? You can have fun coming up with names for them! We used paint pens for ours, but you could also use felt-tip markers, paint sticks, permanent markers, or acrylic paint.

PVA glue seals crafts and will give them a professional-looking finish.
Apply a coat consisting of a mixture of 2 parts PVA to 1 part water using a paintbrush, and let your crafts dry overnight.

MARBLED ROCK PHOTO HOLDERS

This craft makes the ideal gift for a friend or loved one, and adding a photo will give it an extra-personal touch. If you don't have nail polish or yours are too valuable to spare, pick up a few bottles at your local discount store. It's well worth it—the results are really fun!

TOOLS & MATERIALS

- Glass bowl
- Various nail polishes in matte or bold hues
- Rocks (try to find smooth, flat ones with a uniform color and a diameter of at least 2 inches)
- 20-gauge craft wire
- Pliers
- Felt-tip pen

 STEP 1

Fill a large glass bowl with water.

STEP 2

Add blobs of nail polish, one color at a time, working quickly until you like your design.

A glass bowl works best, as you can easily clean off any excess nail polish after finishing the project.

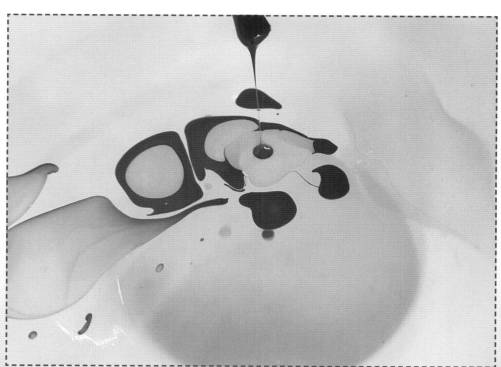

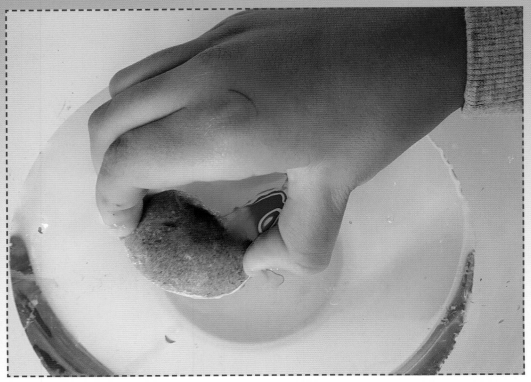

 STEP 3

Dip each rock in the nail polish, ensuring that it is fully submerged. Then place it on newspaper to dry.

STEP 4

Wrap wire around each rock.

STEP 5

Twist the ends of the wire to secure it.

I find it helpful to hold the wire with pliers while my kids twist the rocks.

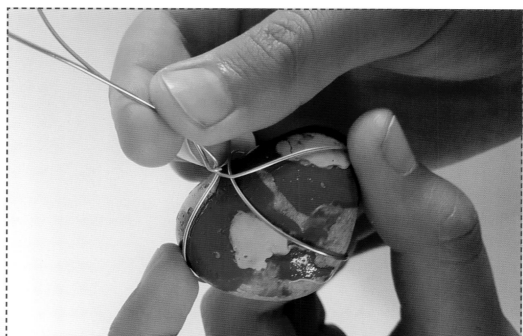

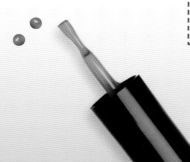

 # STEP 6

Twist the other end of the wire around a felt-tip pen about three times to make the photo holder. Finish by straightening the wire, trimming off any sharp edges, and adding a photo!

Once you've gotten the hang of this technique, you can start experimenting! Try quickly swirling the nail polish with a cocktail stick before dipping the rock or adding marbling to another item—seashells, miniature pumpkins, trinkets, and even mugs work well!

STICK WANDS

My kids and I love the wonderful simplicity of this project, as well as the fact that you can customize it to your heart's content. You may need to help younger children with the tying and cutting, but they'll soon get the hang of the wrapping!

TOOLS & MATERIALS

- Assorted colors of yarn
- Clean, dry stick
- Scissors
- Beads and bells
- Ribbon
- Optional: feathers

STEP 1

Cut a 3-foot piece of yarn and tie one end in a double knot around the top of the stick.

STEP 2

Hold the shorter length of yarn in your hand so that it points downward, and wrap the longer piece of yarn around the stick, gradually working your way down.

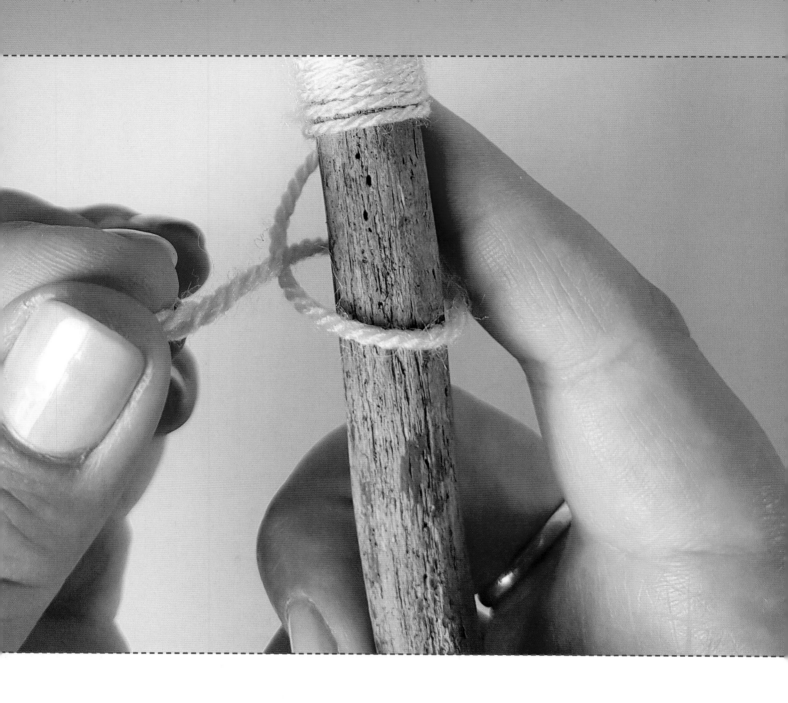

 STEP 3

Once you reach almost to the end of the piece of yarn and have only about 2 inches to spare, loop it around to create a simple knot. Your child may need help with this step!

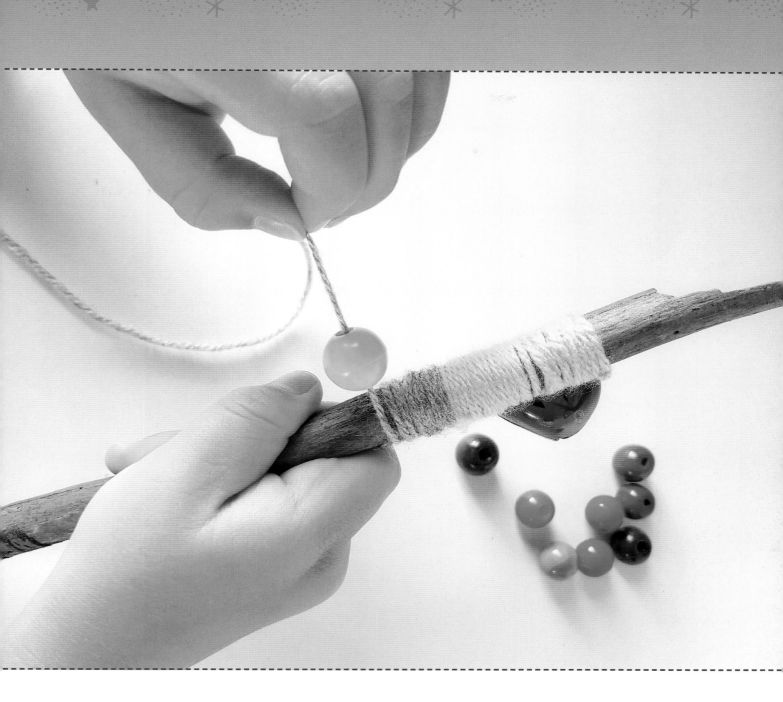

 # STEP 4

Repeat steps 1-3 to add a new color of yarn. Then you can add bells and beads by threading them onto the piece of yarn before wrapping it around a few times to secure. Have your child help choose colors and accessories!

Ensure that any loose threads point downward so that they are covered by the next piece of yarn.

STEP 5

Once you've added your final piece of yarn, secure it to the stick using a double knot and tie on any ribbons you want to add. Add feathers by poking them into the yarn.

If you don't have any beads or feathers on hand, you can still have lots of fun wrapping yarn around sticks. How about making a colorful handle for a marshmallow-toasting stick or adding a few of your nature finds (see pages 12-19)?

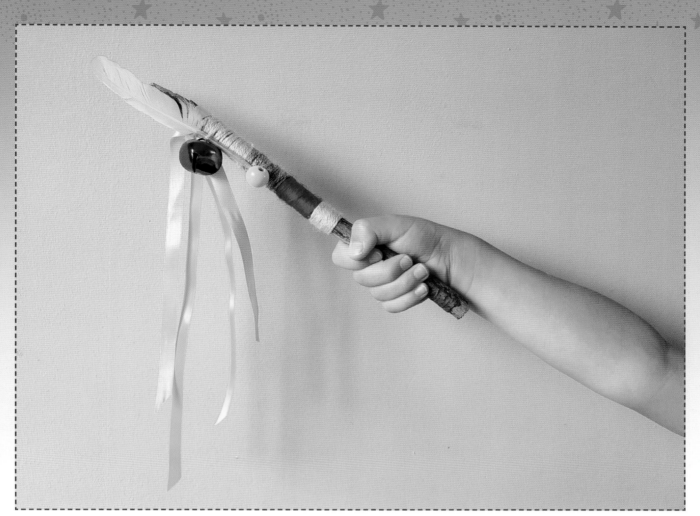

SUN-PRINTED BANNER

The photographic process of making a sun print, or cyanotype, uses chemicals and the sun to create beautiful prints. Here I will show you how you can get similar results using just acrylic paint!

Do this activity on a bright, calm day—the more sun, the better. When choosing your natural materials for printing, try to find leaves and flowers that feature interesting patterns and textures. You will get the best results from plants with softer leaves and flowers with defined petals.

Tools & Materials

- Natural items, such as leaves and flowers
- Dish towel
- Acrylic paints (dark colors work best)
- Water
- Bowl
- Paintbrush
- Paper towel
- Iron
- 2 round dowels or thin sticks
- Fusible web
- Yarn

 **STEP 1**

Collect your leaves and flowers; then thoroughly wet the dish towel and spread it flat on the plastic sheet or tray.

Mix 1 part acrylic paint with 2 parts water. (You can use one color or several, as we did.) Then, using a paintbrush, thoroughly cover the fabric with the paint mixture.

✦✦ STEP 2

Place the flowers and leaves on the fabric and smooth them down with a paintbrush. Leave the fabric in a sunny spot for at least two hours, until the fabric is dry.

STEP 3

Remove the leaves and flowers and admire the beautiful marks they've made!

STEP 4

Ironing is for grown-ups only! Place the piece of fabric between two sheets of paper towel. With your iron on medium heat, iron the fabric for 3 to 4 minutes to set the color. Then rinse the fabric in cold water and hang to dry.

STEP 5

You're now ready to make the banner! Choose your favorite area of the print and cut a rectangle of about 10" × 15".

STEP 6

Wrap the shorter end of the fabric around one of the dowels, creating a hem with the fusible web inside; then iron over the area with medium heat to set. Repeat with the other end of the fabric.

STEP 7

Tie yarn to each end of one of the sticks and hang your banner. If you'd like to add tassels, see pages 125-127 to discover how.

RAINBOW LEAF GARLAND

This is one of the few activities in this book that requires advance planning, as you must press your leaves for a week before painting them. Your kids will have just as much fun painting freshly gathered leaves, but they tend to curl and your garland won't look as good!

TOOLS & MATERIALS

- Leaves
- Various paint colors
- Paintbrush
- PVA glue
- Ribbon

STEP 1

Choose a nice, dry day to collect undamaged leaves. Place the leaves in a flower press or between heavy books for at least one week. Place the leaves between the actual books, not between their pages, as the leaves may damage the pages. Then carefully remove the dried leaves and lay them on newspaper or a tray.

 # STEP 2

Paint the leaves using a rainbow of colors. Acrylic paint will create the boldest results, while watercolors allow the tones of the leaves to show through. Let the paint dry; then cut the stems from the leaves.

 # STEP 3

Overlap one leaf at a time; then glue them all in place.

STEP 4

Tie the ribbon in a bow, leaving a large loop. The easiest way to do this is to tie the ribbon around a cup or mug.

STEP 5

Glue the bow to the top leaf, let the glue dry, and hang your garland to display it!

If you have extra leaves after creating your garland, why not take it one step further and create a wreath as well? You and your kids can follow the same process, except that you will glue the leaves in a circle. The colors don't have to be a rainbow; let kids choose their own favorites!

AROUND THE HOME

So many items in your home can be repurposed for crafting! Consider the crafting potential of items you might be about to discard. Could you save the buttons from old clothes or the spare bolts from your latest DIY project?

Thrift stores are also a great source for household materials. A cheap necklace could provide the beads for your latest craft, and readymade craft kits can be purchased at a fraction of their original price.

Consider how safe an object is before allowing your child to craft with it. Does it have any loose pieces or sharp edges? For example, for younger kids who are prone to putting things in their mouths, you should avoid crafting with beads.

Examples: buttons, beads, clothespins, twine, sponges, nuts and bolts, shoelaces, and corks

Old wine corks are great for making seasonal decorations using just a little felt and card stock.

Plain twine is handy to have in your craft kit, and it can be transformed with a little paint. Liquid watercolors and watered-down acrylics create the most vibrant results. Try wrapping your painted string around a jar and gluing the ends to make a lovely little vase.

Use masking or washi tape to hold the string in place until the glue is dry.

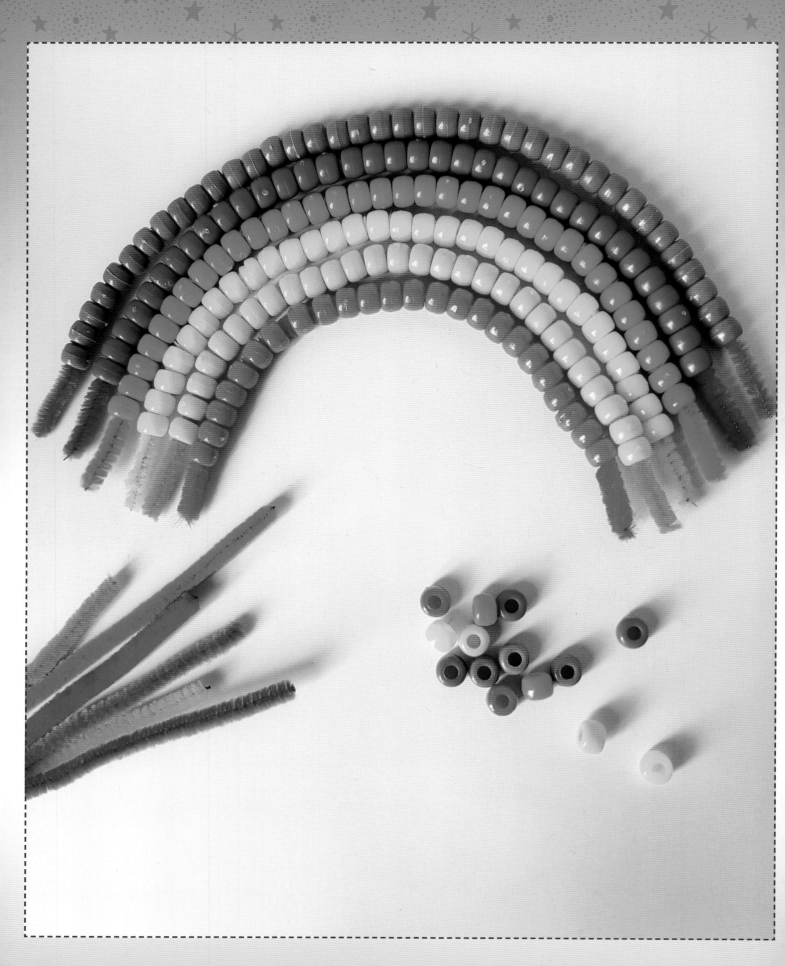

You can make a wide variety of decorations by threading pony beads onto pipe cleaners. Snowflakes, hearts, pumpkins, and stars are simple to make by even the littlest of hands. Just fold over any sharp ends, and when you're finished, you can secure the beads in place by twisting the pipe cleaners together.

Use beads with larger holes—1/8 inch should suffice.

How cute is this button bracelet? It's unbelievably simple to make! Push a pipe cleaner through one buttonhole, and then double back through another. Keep adding buttons until the bracelet is long enough to go around a wrist; then twist the ends together to secure.

Buttons are one of our favorite crafting resources—they can be used for so many things! Making your own greetings cards is a lovely, simple way to get into crafting—think balloons, fairy lights, baubles, and flowers. Glue them on with PVA and, once dry, add details with a marker.

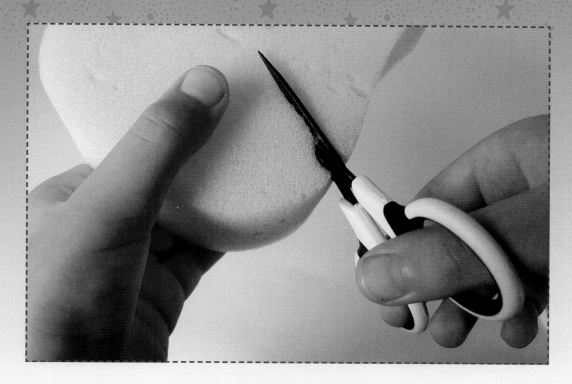

This fun idea—transforming cheap sponges into toy cakes—is perfect for hosting a teddy bear's tea party! My children and I are huge fans of pretend food; it's great for imaginary play. We made the icing on the layer cake from equal amounts of PVA glue and white acrylic paint mixed together, and the pink frosting came from a tube of glitter glue. Apply liberally and let dry overnight for a great frosted-cake effect.

Plain wooden clothespins make a fun addition to your craft supplies. Why not invite your child to design a dinosaur, and then make it come to life with colorful paper and painted clothespins for spikes? The beauty of this craft is that the spikes can be taken on and off, so your child can decide how many to include.

Here we painted clothespins to make a friendly spider. We drew the eyes with permanent marker, but you could also use stickers or paint. Thumbprints are another fun way for little ones to make eyes. Use a thumb for the white of the eye and a smaller finger for the pupil.

You can also use clothespins to make legs for a giraffe, ears for a rabbit, or the body of a butterfly.

CLAY ROBOTS

TOOLS & MATERIALS

- Air-dry modeling clay
- Nuts and bolts
- Silver beads (mine came from an old necklace)
- Any other metal parts you can find, such as cogs, key fobs, washers, and springs

I love this craft—not only is it incredibly easy to set up once you've collected a handful of metallic or silver loose parts, but it also has a wonderful sensory element to it. Kids will have so much fun molding clay and choosing features for their little robot creations. You'll want to work on a tray and get out a full-size apron (see page 7) for this project; the clay is washable, but it can get messy, and covering yourself and your work surface will make cleanup much easier.

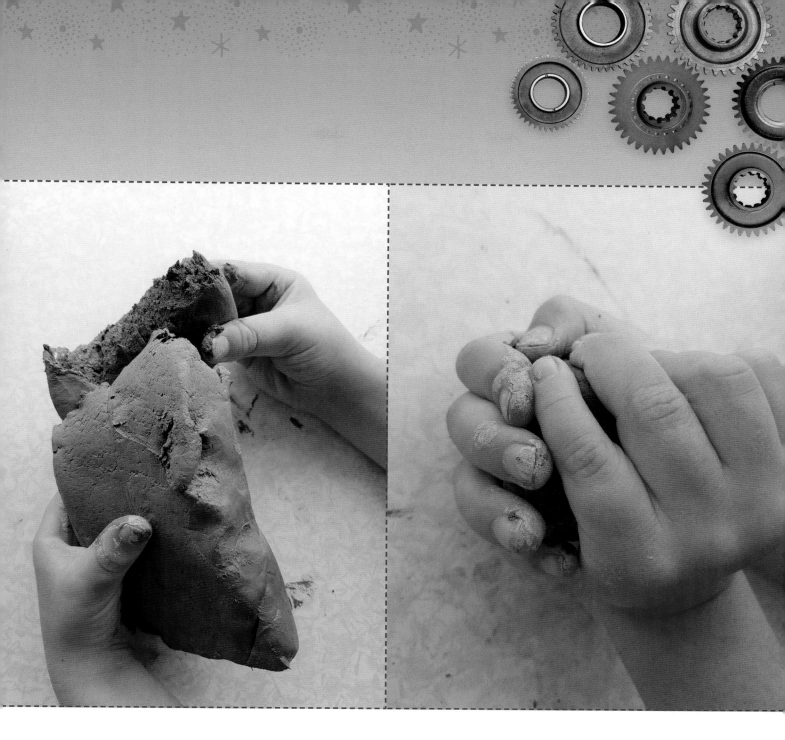

 # STEP 1

Tear off a chunk of clay, and wrap the remainder to save for another project. Your child can squish the clay to soften it. You don't have to add water, but moist clay is easier to work with.

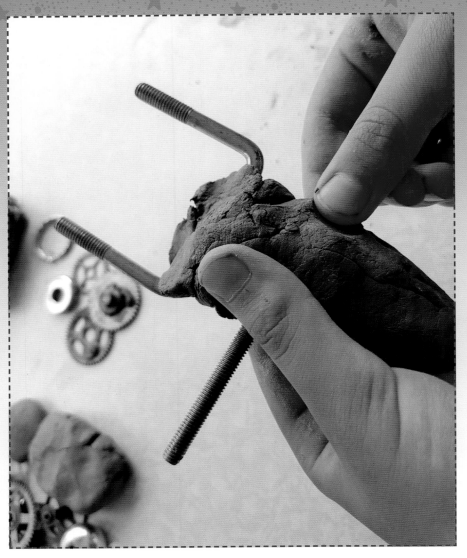

STEP 2

Create the rough shape of a robot; then add features, such as arms made from screws and beads for eyes.

Kids can really let their imaginations run wild here!

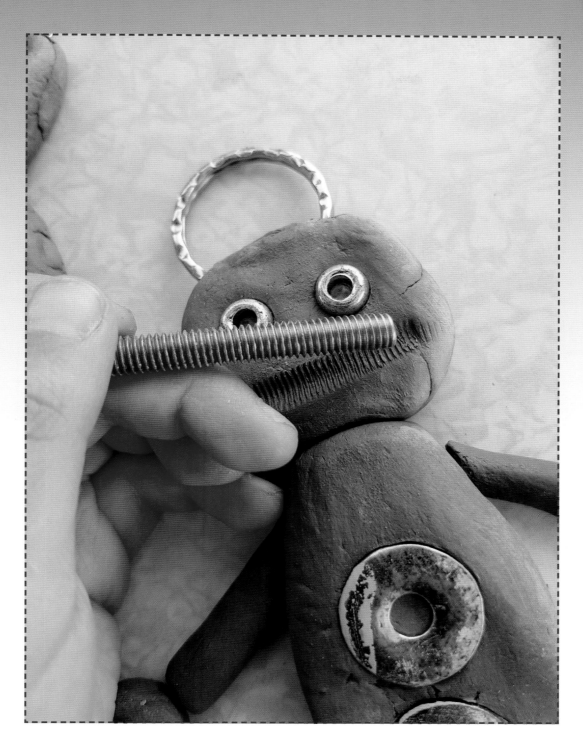

*⁺✦ STEP 3

Encourage your child to explore the textures of the various objects, and have fun using them to create prints and patterns!

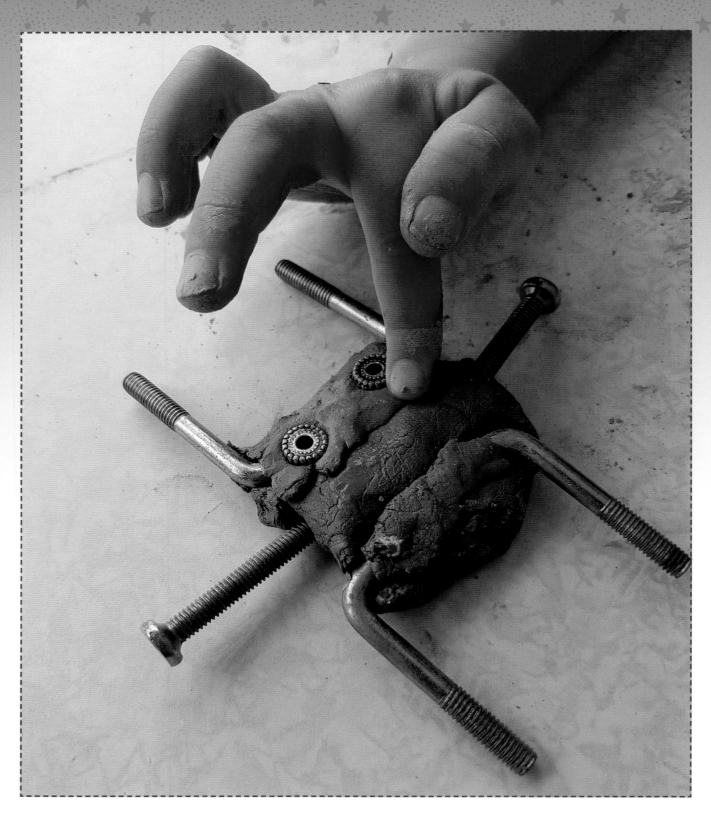

 STEP 4

Have your child dip their fingers in water and smooth down
any rough patches or cracks in the robot.

 # STEP 5

Let the robot dry overnight. You can leave it as is, or you may want to add paint once the clay is completely dry.

Acrylic paints will give you the best finish over clay.

CLOTHESPIN BUTTERFLY

This cute activity is quick and easy for even the youngest of crafters, as well as a group of kids working together. All you need are a couple of household items, pipe cleaners, glue, and pens.

TOOLS & MATERIALS

- 2 white cupcake liners
- Paintbrush
- PVA glue
- Felt-tip pens
- Plain wooden clothespin
- Pipe cleaners
- Scissors

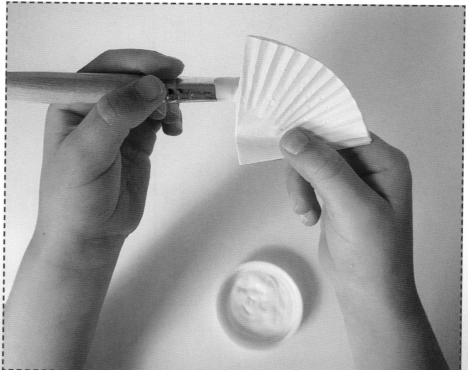

 **STEP 1**

Fold each cupcake liner in half twice and glue it in the middle. Repeat with a second liner.

✳ STEP 2

Use felt-tip pens to add color to the cupcake liners, which will form the butterflies' wings. You can try patterns, spots, stripes, multiple colors, or even a more realistic-looking butterfly-wing pattern. Then color a clothespin.

STEP 3

Glue the wings together so they resemble a bow tie.

STEP 4

Cut the pipe cleaner in half, fold it in half to create a "V" shape, and then wrap the ends around a finger to curl. This will form the butterfly's antennae.

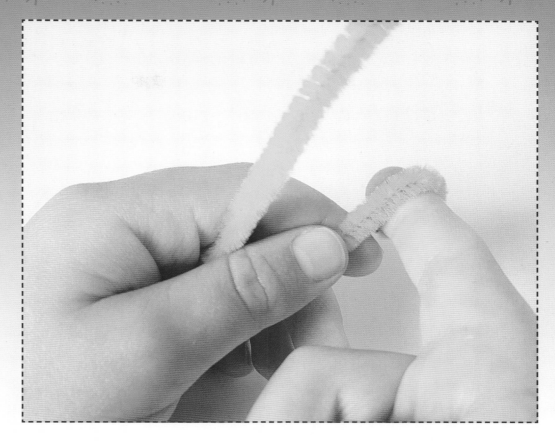

STEP 5

Open the clothespin and add some glue, place the wings and antennae inside, and let it dry.

To create a caterpillar to go with your butterfly, simply glue green pom-poms on another clothespin and give it some googly eyes!

JELLYFISH SUNCATCHER

This craft looks beautiful on a wall or against a window with the light shining through! Once you've learned the technique, you can make any shape of suncatcher. We've made lots of favorite book characters and seasonal decorations following this process.

TOOLS & MATERIALS

- Small plate (for tracing)
- White card stock
- Scissors
- Tissue paper in various colors
- Self-adhesive contact paper
- Stapler or glue
- Anything you have at home that will make good tentacles; we used curling ribbon, strips of bubble wrap, twine, and a paper towel

When crafting with younger children, I recommend that an adult prep steps 1-4 in advance, so the kids can go straight to sticking on the squares of tissue paper.

✦ STEP 1

Trace the top half of a plate onto a sheet of card stock, and draw a wiggly line along the bottom. Then draw a line about 1 inch in from the curved line. This will create your jellyfish outline.

✦ STEP 2

Use sharp scissors to carefully cut out your shape.

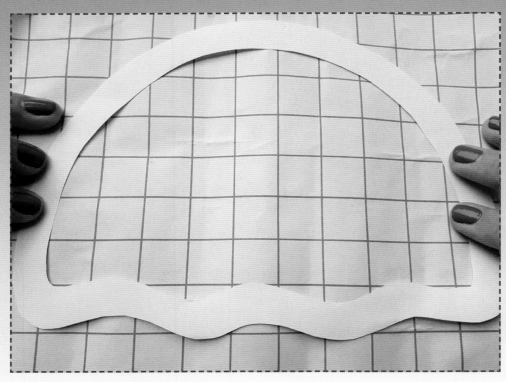

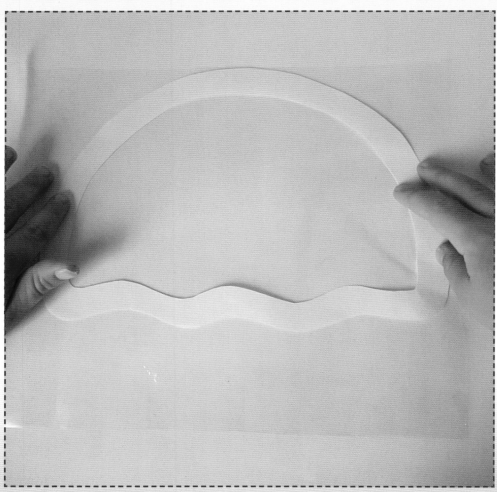

Cut a square of contact paper to fit the area of the jellyfish, remove the backing, and adhere the jellyfish to the paper.

STEP 4

Cut a selection of tissue paper into 1-inch squares. The easiest way to do this is to fold the paper in half five times and trim off the edges.

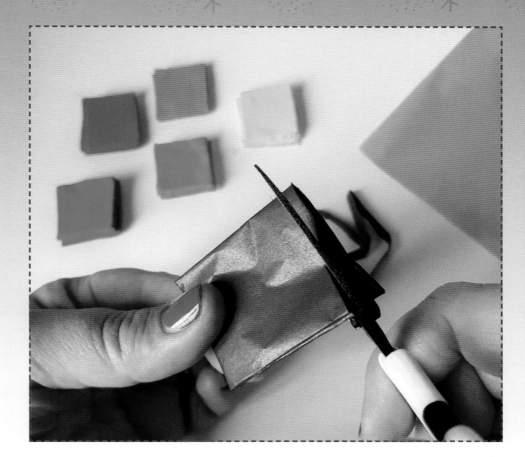

STEP 5

With the adhesive side of the contact paper up, add the tissue paper one square at a time, ensuring that the squares overlap slightly. Try to avoid interfering when your kids complete this step—if they want to place a bunch of colors in one area, let them! It's all part of the charm, and it's better that they have something to be proud of that they created independently than a perfect-looking craft.

 STEP 6

When the jellyfish is covered in tissue paper, cut around the outside and trim off any excess tissue paper (anything that goes over the edges of the card stock).

 # STEP 7

Select the materials for your tentacles and cut them to about 12 inches long.

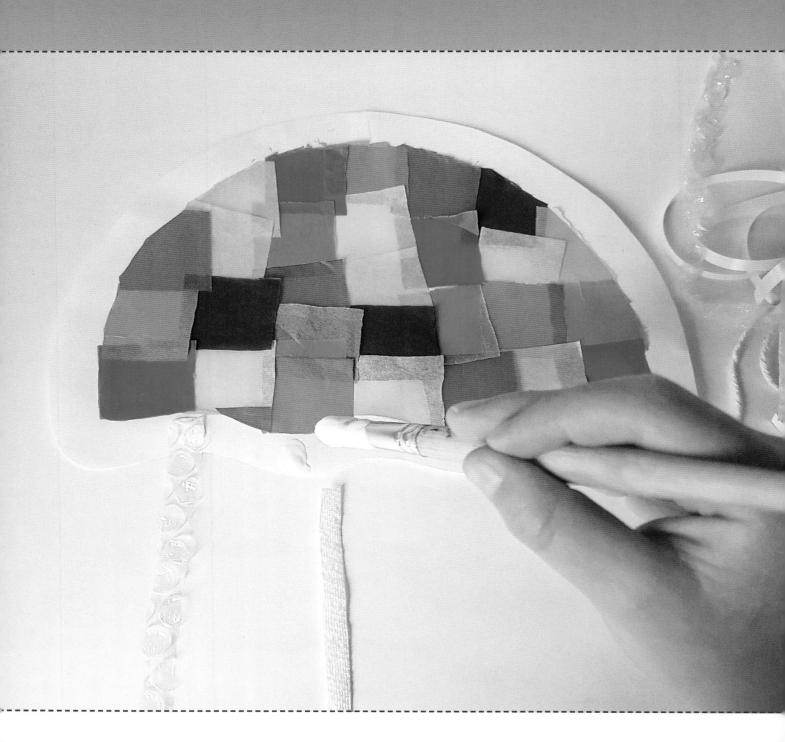

 # STEP 8

Now you can attach your tentacles to the jellyfish. The quickest way to do this is to staple the tentacles to the bottom of the jellyfish. If you have a bit more time to spare (and the patience!), you can use glue instead. Then, once the glue is dry, adhere your jellyfish to a window or hang it from the ceiling using thread.

RECYCLING

Recycled packaging is a great source of free crafting materials. Even an empty cereal box or a plastic bottle can make for some amazing creations. Whether working with plastic, wood, paper, or cardboard, kids will love spotting the potential in any item.

It's easy and quick to build up a collection of recycled objects; we keep a container near our recycling bin and regularly add items to it. When my children are in the mood for a crafting session, we raid the container to see what we can use!

Examples: plastic spoons, water bottles, lollipop sticks, cereal boxes, aluminum foil, wooden coffee stirrers, lids, straws, jars, and magazine cutouts

It didn't take us long to build up this collection; we just separated out items with interesting shapes or colors before adding to our recycling bin, cleaning and drying everything before storing. If you don't have the space to store larger pieces of packaging, toss them in the recycling bin and keep only smaller items like lids. Crafting with recycled materials is a great way to avoid discarding single-use plastic packaging.

One of the most versatile recycled materials is cardboard. It's easy to cut, it can be transformed with just a bit of paint, and it's readily available. It's also perfect for making toys. This castle has given my children hours of entertainment, and it was made using just a cereal box and paper towel rolls!

To make the castle walls, we used four equal-sized rectangles from a cereal box. We cut out some battlements, which we painted gray, and then added a little brick detailing using a sponge and lighter gray paint. The paper towel towers have slits in them so that the whole thing can be slotted together. You can even pack away the entire castle once your kids are done playing with it!

Cardboard tubes are an incredibly useful crafting material—you can find whole books on their uses! How about trying a little stacking toy? To make it stack, you just need to cut four slits in each end.

We made this lovely lion from a paper plate. You could also make a cat, bear, tiger, or dog using different colors of paint and yarn.

A craft knife and cutting mat will come in handy when cutting awkward shapes, such as cardboard tubes.

Although it can be a little time consuming, building up a supply of paper cutouts is worth the effort. Cutouts can come from magazines, brochures, greetings cards, wrapping paper, and anything else with an interesting picture or bold colors. Before recycling magazines, I tear out the pages that I like and, when I have the chance, I'll grab my scissors and add to our collection. I find it to be a therapeutic activity with a cup of coffee on the side!

We also have a collection of colorful paper; any nice wrapping paper, napkins, and wallpaper samples make it into a small tub ready for our crafting projects. I always try to use these before buying new paper for a craft.

Decant glue into a small jar or recycled tub so that your child doesn't overuse it.

MAGAZINE PLANT POTS

This craft is super simple to prep. If you choose easy-to-care-for plants such as succulents, it's also a great way to introduce kids to gardening. You will need about 15 to 20 pictures. We used cutouts of plants and flowers from gardening magazines. Older children may prefer to cut out their own pictures, but I would recommend preparing the pictures in advance if you're working with younger children. If you want to keep your pot outside, you will need to seal the finished pot with a clear varnish.

Tools & Materials

- Magazine cutouts
- PVA glue
- Paintbrush
- Small terra-cotta pot
- Small plant

STEP 1

Carefully cut out pictures from your magazine(s) of choice. Aim to use pictures that are no larger than 2 inches in diameter; if the pictures are too big, you will struggle to get a smooth finish. Then spread glue on the back of each picture, stick it on the pot, and add a little more glue on top.

STEP 2

Repeat with the remaining pictures. Don't worry if they overlap—it's all part of the appeal!

STEP 3

Trim any edges that stick out.

STEP 4

Once the pictures are dry, seal the whole surface of the pot with a thin layer of glue.

 # STEP 5

Let the glue dry, and then varnish the pot if you plan to keep it outside.

This process of covering objects with cut or torn paper is called "decoupage," and it can be totally addictive—you have been warned! Virtually anything can be decoupaged, and any thin paper or fabric will do. How about transforming a plain photo frame with a child's favorite television character or using napkins and an aluminum can to make a pretty pencil holder? I've even decoupaged a table with comics for my sons. (I covered it with clear polyurethane spray to make it more durable!)

TREASURE BOX

You can also decoupage (see page 83) with gift wrap to make treasure boxes. If your kids are anything like mine, they can never have too many places to store their little treasures, and this is the perfect home for valued possessions such as nature finds, stationery, and trinkets! Anything colorful and shiny can be used for decoration; we even added some candy wrappers!

Tools & Materials

- Gift wrap
- PVA glue
- Paintbrush
- Small cardboard box with a lid (such as a child's shoebox)
- Scissors
- Gems, sequins, and shiny buttons

STEP 1

Rip pieces of gift wrap into roughly 2-inch squares.

STEP 2

Spread glue on the back of each piece of gift wrap and stick it in place. Repeat until you've covered the box.

 STEP 3

Spread another thin layer of glue over the entire surface of the box to flatten any bits of paper that stick up and to create a glossy finish. Let the glue dry.

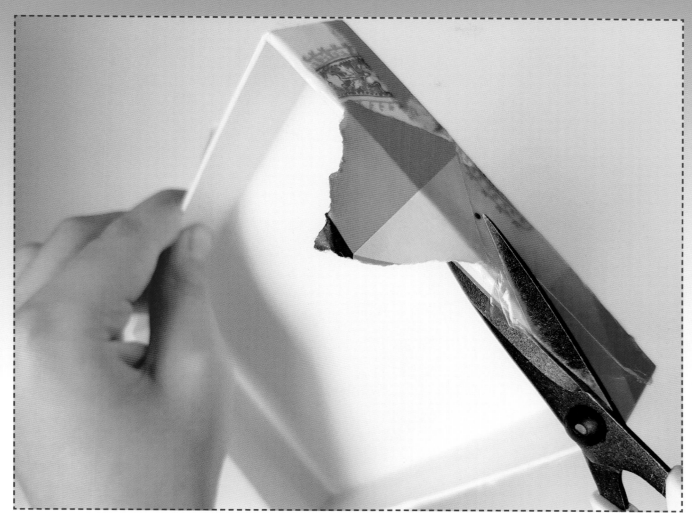

Once dry, trim off any pieces of paper
that stick out from the edges of the box.

✴ STEP 5

Now you and your kids can start decorating! Glue on the
gems, sequins, buttons, and so on, using any design you like.

You don't have to use wrapping paper for your treasure box—let your imagination run wild! Maybe kids would like to make a pirate's treasure chest using brown paper and gold ribbon, or paint some pasta shells and create a treasure box fit for a mermaid.

PAPIER-MÂCHÉ ROCKET

True papier-mâché uses newspaper and a mixture of water and flour as the glue to create a solid finish that's easy to paint over. This rocket makes a fun toy, or you can hang it from the ceiling and use it as room décor!

TOOLS & MATERIALS

- Flour
- Hot water
- Masking tape
- Newspaper
- Small plastic bottle
- Cardboard
- Acrylic paints
- Paintbrush
- Washi tape
- Optional: stickers
- String (to hang your rocket)

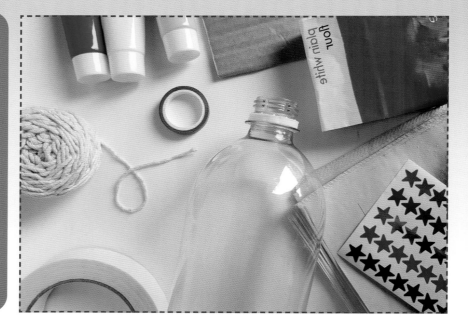

*★ STEP 1

Start by making your papier-mâché paste. Add 4 or 5 tablespoons of flour to a bowl and gradually whisk in hot (but not boiling) water until the paste has the consistency of heavy cream. Cover and set aside.

STEP 2

Smooth masking tape over the top of the bottle to give it a rocket shape. Pull the tape nice and taut.

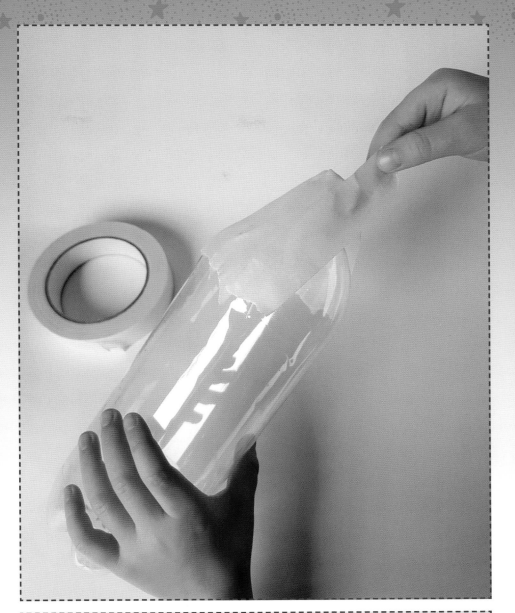

STEP 3

Tear the newspaper into ½-inch-wide strips.

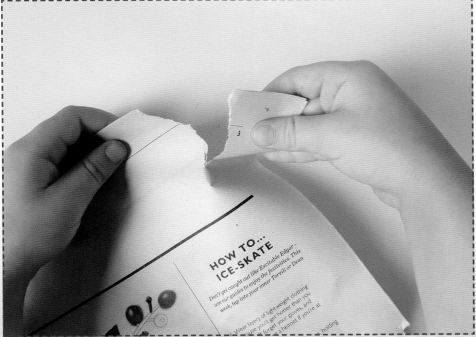

STEP 4

Dipping the strips in the paste as you go and letting any excess run off, cover the bottle with strips. Overlap them until you've completely covered the bottle; then let it dry.

STEP 5

Draw three fin shapes on the cardboard and cut them out; then cut a small slit in the straight side of each fin and fold in the opposite way.

STEP 6

Use masking tape to attach the fins to the rocket.

STEP 7

Now you can have fun painting and decorating your rocket! We used acrylic paint and then added details with star stickers and washi tape.

Once you've mastered the papier-mâché technique, its uses are limitless! How about hanging a fish from a rod or covering half of a balloon and popping it when dry to create a bowl? To make freeform shapes, crumple up aluminum foil, use masking tape to smooth out the shape, and cover it in papier-mâché. We have made many items using this method, including props for our school nativity scene and a tennis racket for a homework project.

TEXTILES

The term "textile" covers anything woven, knit, or made from fiber. Textiles are affordable and can come from leftover sewing fabric, an unraveled sweater, or old clothing. Blankets, reusable cloth bags, and curtains can all be repurposed. Thrift stores and online auction sites make good sources for materials too. Alternatively, I recommend visiting your local craft store and picking up small packages of mixed textiles. As with our paper supplies (page 74), I keep a plastic tub filled with fabric for crafting.

Examples: ribbon, yarn, felt, cotton, thread, silk, lace, velvet, and rope

This colorful selection of yarn came from an online auction site and could be used for so many things. We always have a small supply in a mixture of colors, and I pop any leftover fabric into an old takeout container so that we don't waste anything.

Kids can use these little pom-pom monsters to help express themselves as they choose colors and features for their creatures. There's a pom-pom tutorial starting on page 108 if you'd like to make your own, or you can pick up affordable sets of mixed pom-poms. My oldest son decided to create pipe-cleaner horns and a pom-pom nose for his creature, while his brother opted for giant pointy teeth.

This paper-plate suncatcher is a pretty way to use leftover yarn; you only need a 4-foot piece of yarn to create it.

Start by cutting out the center of a paper plate; then use a single hole punch or pencil to make eight equally spaced holes.

To create a more traditional pattern, thread the yarn through each hole. Then, when you're back to where you started, pass the yarn through the gap in each of the adjoining lines of yarn, one at a time, working in a clockwise direction. Once you get to the center, pull the yarn tight and tie in a knot to secure. Younger children can make a more free-form design by randomly threading the yarn through the holes.

Socks can be used to make stuffed animals; all you need is cotton wool for filling. It's much easier than sewing, and you can create a unique cuddle buddy for your child! Ask your children what animals they can make from leftover socks.

My son and I made this bunny together when he was two years old, and she is well loved! We stuffed a sock from the heel until half full, created a head using a rubber band and some more stuffing, and then cut the top of the sock in half lengthwise to make the ears.

You could also make a "socktopus" using the same method. Stuff the toe-end of a sock and twist a rubber band around the sock to make the body. Cut off the elastic at the top of the sock, cut the end into eight strips, and finish with googly eyes!

Our crafting supplies include various colors of ribbon. Some of these we purchased, some we saved from gifts, and some came from boxes of chocolates! Ribbon isn't the cheapest crafting material out there, but you can make many beautiful things from it, so it's well worth having a small supply.

We made this rainbow by gluing ribbons to a cloud shape cut from white card stock and covered in cotton wool.

Scrap-fabric bowls are lots of fun to create—all you need is fabric-stiffening glue! Apply liberally to your fabric, scrape off any excess, and mold the fabric around a glass or plastic bowl. Let it dry completely before peeling off. This technique works well on any type of material, but keep in mind that thicker fabrics, such as velvet and corduroy, will be harder to shape.

Pinking shears are a good investment; they stop material from fraying and can add pretty edges to greeting cards.

The versatility of felt makes it my favorite textile for crafting. You can use it to create so many things! We made these little brooches by cutting out pieces of felt, gluing them together with PVA, and attaching a safety pin. You and your kids can design your brooches together, or choose one of the numerous templates online.

Small, sharp scissors work best when cutting felt.

NO-SEW FELT FLOWERS

TOOLS & MATERIALS

- Chalk marker or tailor's chalk
- Various colors of felt
- Scissors
- Buttons
- PVA glue
- Paintbrush
- Garden stakes or skewers painted green
- Optional: dark green felt

There are many tutorials online for making felt flowers, but most require some sewing skills or a die-cut machine. The beauty of these flowers is that you only need a pair of sharp scissors and some PVA glue, and they are so simple that children of all ages can create them. They make the perfect Mother's Day gift or a fun toy for playing in the garden. Make just one or a whole bunch!

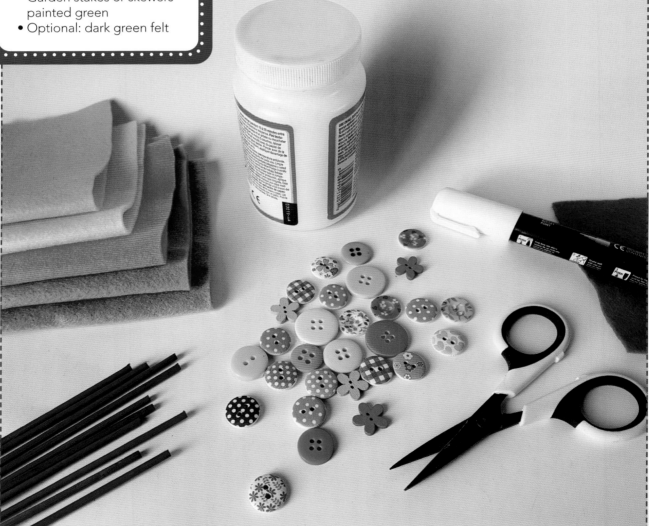

STEP 1

Use your chalk marker or tailor's chalk to draw floral shapes and circles on the colored felt; then cut out the shapes. If you're crafting with younger children, you may want to prep this step in advance!

STEP 2

Place a circle and then a button on top of each flower, choosing contrasting color combinations.

STEP 3

Glue the two felt parts together; then glue a button on top. Let dry.

STEP 4

Glue a garden stake or
skewer to the back of
each flower.

STEP 5

If you'd like to add leaves to
your flowers, fold a small piece
of green felt in half and cut a
teardrop shape from it; then
glue the shape to the stick.

I used a simple floral shape in this project, but you should feel free
to cut your flowers any way you like. An alternative to felt leaves is ribbon,
which you can tie around the stem in a bow.

POM-POMS

Tools & Materials

- Pom-pom-making set (see "Introduction" to the right)
- Yarn
- Craft scissors

This crafting skill is well worth learning! Not only is it fun to make and play with pom-poms in all sizes and colors, but you can also create so many things with them—think animals, holiday decorations, bag charms, and so on. They can be made from DIY cardboard rings, but this is quite time-consuming, so I recommend investing in a pom-pom-making set. You can find affordable ones on the internet. Mine came in a set with three different sizes of plastic rings; pictured here is the largest of the three sets.

STEP 1

Pull out one of the double-sided parts of the ring and tie the end of the yarn to the left side.

STEP 2

Wrap the yarn in a continuous loop around half of the ring, carefully working from left to right, until you've covered the whole thing. Do this in the opposite direction and then back again (3 times total) until half of the ring is generously covered in yarn. The more yarn you wrap, the fuller your pom-pom will be.

✦ STEP 3

When half of the ring is full, close it and open the other side, passing the yarn through the opening.

✦ STEP 4

Cover the second half of the ring in the same way you covered the first; then close that side. Using the opening to guide your sharp craft scissors, cut through the center of the yarn, around the ring. Younger children will need your help with this step.

✦ STEP 5

Cut a piece of yarn and place it around the middle. Tie it as tightly as you can, using one knot and then another one to secure it.

✦ STEP 6

Carefully open each half of the ring; then pull apart the center piece.

 # STEP 7

If any of the pieces of yarn look too long, snip them to create an even, tidy-looking pom-pom shape.

And there you have it! Pom-poms may seem tricky at first, but once you've done it a couple of times, you will be a pom-pom wiz! Younger children will need some help with the cutting, but they will soon get the hang of the wrapping; try starting with smaller pom-poms, as they require less yarn and are quicker to make.

You can use this project to create the pom-pom ice-cream cone on pages 114-121.

POM-POM ICE-CREAM CONES

Once you've mastered making pom-poms (pages 108-113), you can have fun setting up your own ice-cream parlor with this super-cool craft!

Tools & Materials

- Light-brown card stock or thick paper
- Scissors
- Brown felt-tip pen
- Plate
- Pencil
- Double-sided tape
- PVA glue
- Large pom-pom

STEP 1

Measure 4½ inches in from the edges of the card stock or paper and draw lines in pencil to form a square.

STEP 2

Cut out the square.

STEP 3

Use brown pen to draw lines every ½ inch, creating a grid.

STEP 4

Place a plate between two of the corners in the square and use a pencil to trace around the plate. Cut along the line to cut off a corner of the square.

STEP 5

Cut a length of double-sided tape and place it along one of the straight inside edges.

STEP 6

Peel back the tape and use it to join the edges of the card stock or paper.

STEP 7

Spread glue around the top of the ice-cream cone, place the pom-pom on top, and press firmly. Leave to dry.

TAPE-RESIST BOOKMARKS

This is the perfect craft for any little bookworms in your home! Tape resist never fails to delight, and kids love the big reveal at the end, when their geometric paintings "magically" appear.

TOOLS & MATERIALS

- Washi tape
- White card stock
- Scissors
- Acrylic paints
- Credit card or another item of a similar size
- Colored yarn
- Single hole punch

Place a tray or newspaper over your creative space before getting started, just in case your child paints over the sides of the card stock.

STEP 1

Add strips of washi tape to a sheet of card stock—the more abstract the better! Consider adding details, such as lots of pieces of tape right next to each other or curved pieces of tape. To curve the tape, pull it to stretch while pressing it in place with your other hand. The great thing about washi tape is that you can tear it to size, but younger children may need help with using scissors to cut their tape.

STEP 2

Paint section by section until the whole area is covered. You and your kids can use as many or as few colors as you like!

 # STEP 3

Now you and your kids can have fun seeing the beautiful patterns you made together! Carefully peel off all of the pieces of tape; then select an area of the card stock to cut into a 2" x 6" bookmark.

STEP 4

Using a credit card or another item, gently wrap yarn all the way around the long side about 15 times (chunkier yarns will require less wrapping). Make sure you stop at the same end where you started.

STEP 5

Cut a 6-inch piece of yarn and, opposite from where you started and finished wrapping the yarn around the card, pass the piece of yarn through the wrapped yarn and tie it in a double knot at the top. Younger children will need a little help with this step!

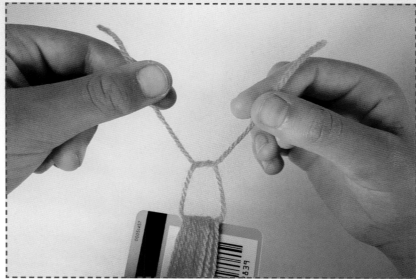

STEP 6

Cut through the yarn opposite from the knot and remove it from the card.

✱ STEP 7

Cut another piece of yarn, gather the tassel, and tie the yarn in a double knot around the tassel, about ½ inch from the top. Trim any uneven pieces of yarn.

✱ STEP 8

Using your single hole punch, create a hole in the bookmark, thread your tassel through, and secure with a double knot. Then pop your finished bookmark into your favorite book!

ABOUT THE ARTIST

Vicki Manning lives with her husband and three boys in rural Oxfordshire, England. She has always had a passion for crafting and loves spending her spare time coming up with engaging and fun activities for her children. To see their creative learning, visit Vicki's Instagram account @howweplayandlearn.

ALSO IN THIS SERIES

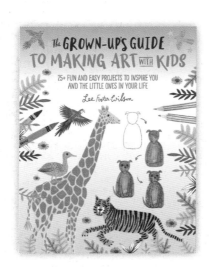

**The Grown-Up's Guide
to Making Art with Kids**

978-1-63322-739-2

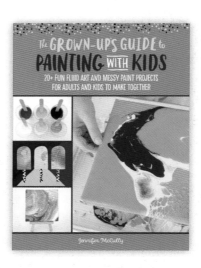

**The Grown-Up's Guide
to Painting with Kids**

978-1-63322-854-2